Finding what was never lost

Finding what was never lost

A pocket guide for spiritual insight and inspiration.

© 2024 Alexander den Heijer

All rights reserved. This book or any portion thereof may not be reproduced or used in any manner whatsoever without the express written permission of the publisher except for the use of brief quotations in a book review.

Book & cover design by Manon Binkhorst

Editing by Julia Willard

Photo by Daisy Duin

ISBN: 9798878120555

www.alexanderdenheijer.com

".. and the end of all our exploring will be to arrive where we started and know the place for the first time."

– T. S. Eliot[1]

Acknowledgments

I'm grateful to many who have shaped my spiritual quest. Special thanks to my friend and mentor, Niek, whom I met in Amsterdam in September 2016. The countless hours of dialogue until his passing in 2020 profoundly affected me. I also thank my friend Zigy van Scheppingen for introducing me to Vipassana meditation in 2017, which has become a cornerstone in my daily life. I honor the late S.N. Goenka and his assistant teachers for their guidance and wisdom.

Gratitude is due to those who reviewed the manuscript: Joyce van Oosterhout, for her thoughtful feedback and support; Bart Biermasz, for his contributions; my friend Martijn Schirp, for his philosophical depth and insightful suggestions. Julia Willard deserves recognition too for her editorial suggestions, and Manon Binkhorst for her creative work on the book's cover and layout. I also thank my friend Ferry de Wit for our fruitful dialogues, and for being a true companion on the spiritual path.

A special thanks goes to The Embassy of the Free Mind in Amsterdam, a wellspring of inspiration that feels like a spiritual home to me. I spent countless hours reading, reflecting, and writing in their library. I am also thankful to everyone at Creative Grounds for providing a great place for my writing as well. Finally, I would like to thank my teachers and peers at Phoenix Opleidingen, where I began a life-altering educational journey in 2022.

Introduction

The subject matter of this book is very dear to me, as the words contained within these pages serve as an external reflection of my ongoing spiritual exploration.

The title of the book refers to that which all spiritual seekers are searching for. It goes by many names, and yet no words can express it. Those who have found it have referred to it as Nirvana, Moksha, the grace of God, enlightenment, salvation, or simply "Home."

Most of the teachings presented in this book are not new; some are very old, older than the written word. Some of these timeless insights can be found throughout various spiritual traditions across the globe.

In our modern era, there exists a dominant belief that the past is inferior to the present; that the new always surpasses the old. And while many people are obsessed with the incredible innovations of our age, the question that interests me is: "But what have we forgotten?"

Many of us have lost sight of the profound wisdom embedded within the great traditions of our ancestors. My aspiration is to restore a little bit of what I think has been lost in our time. In this way, this book can be seen as ancient wisdom for modern day people.

When I was a young adolescent, my soul was extremely restless. A long-time friend of mine told me recently that he often felt nervous merely by being in my presence. Even in a movie theater, where we sat in the dark, he could sense my restlessness.

I remember being profoundly moved by Eckhart Tolle's *The Power of Now*, the first spiritual book I read some 15 years ago. It marked the beginning of my spiritual quest. Tolle's teachings have deeply influenced me.

At the time, I found myself dissatisfied with both the scientific worldview, as well as the Christian worldview I was taught at school. I refused to think that we are merely a bunch of atoms randomly put together with no purpose, nor did I believe in some man with a beard in the sky watching over everything we did.

I started exploring spiritual traditions such as Buddhism, Zen, Taoism, Vedanta, and Sufism. The more exotic the better. I also delved into psychology, philosophy and mythology. I became deeply influenced by the works of Carl Jung, Erich Fromm, Iain McGilchrist, Rupert Spira, Bernardo Kastrup, and many more. I found a mentor, started meditating, and went through psychoanalysis.

Many years later, through thinkers such as Andreas Kinneging, Jordan Peterson, and mystics like Meister Eckhart, I found a renewed interest in my own cultural heritage. I started reading the Bible again, this time with an open mind. Statements like "Be still and know that I am God"[2] were no longer met with suspicion, but with a deep appreciation as they reminded me of the inexplainable peace I had often experienced in meditation retreats. Today I consider myself spiritual in the broadest sense of the word. I do not identify myself with any particular tradition.

The word "spiritual" has many connotations these days. To me, the aim of a spiritual practice is to (re-)connect to our essence, and live in harmony with it. I believe this is also the purpose of an authentic religion as the word "religion" comes from the Latin *religare* which means to "re-connect."

Although I write about spirituality, I must admit I am not particularly interested in spirituality per se. I am interested in the nature of reality. It seems to me that the universe is fundamentally experiential, not material. In other words, the Universe seems more like an orchestra than a bunch of objects. There's harmony and dissonance, cycles and seasons, patterns and rhythms. Everything is connected to everything else. Like a universal song or verse; the *uni-verse*.

The most important implication of an experiential universe is that consciousness is the fundamental reality, because all experience appears in consciousness, and is known by it. Throughout this book, I use the words consciousness and awareness interchangeably.

The seven chapters in this book reflect different stages of the spiritual path. Like my previous book *Nothing you don't already know*, you can open this book to any page and find an insight to reflect on. Some pages will contain practical ideas and insights, whereas others are more like meditations or contemplations. You can also read it from start to finish as the book will take you on a journey from suffering to serenity.

Coincidentally, each chapter of this book starts with the letter S. A friend of mine, after noticing this, made me aware that the letter S refers to the Hebrew letter Shin, which is derived from an ancient glyph that represents a tooth. This lovely coincidence put a smile on my face. Why? A tooth symbolizes the transformation (chewing) of raw material into something usable and digestible. This entire book is the result of my endless chewing on complex ideas and insights in order to transform them into digestible nuggets that are useful for people on their spiritual path.

You can see this book as a companion on your spiritual path. Written, not by some enlightened guru, but by a spiritual friend who has been walking a similar path.

My hope for this book is that it will (re)awaken in you a recognition of your essence, and that it may inspire you to bring forth the love, truth and beauty that resides within you, as you.

Alexander

Contents

14 Suffering
36 Sincerity
52 Stillness
70 Surrender
92 Shift
112 Simplicity
128 Serenity

Suffering

"This being human is a guest house.
Every morning a new arrival.

A joy, a depression, a meanness,
some momentary awareness comes
as an unexpected visitor.

Welcome and entertain them all!
Even if they're a crowd of sorrows,
who violently sweep your house
empty of its furniture,
still, treat each guest honorably.
He may be clearing you out
for some new delight.

The dark thought, the shame, the malice,
meet them at the door laughing,
and invite them in.

Be grateful for whoever comes,
because each has been sent
as a guide from beyond."

— Rumi[3]

The belief that we must always feel positive generates negativity.

According to the Buddha, suffering is one of the fundamental realities of life, which he identified as the first noble truth. Accepting this fact can be a great relief, particularly in a society that promotes the idea that we must constantly be happy.

The word that the Buddha used that is commonly translated as suffering, is *duhkha*, but it more specifically refers to a sense of discontentment or unease. *Duhkha* is the basic condition many of us live in.

Our attachment to pleasant experiences and our aversion to unpleasant ones is the primary reason for this sense of unease. It leads to a constant cycle of craving the pleasant while resisting the unpleasant, which produces endless unease.

In an effort to alleviate this unease, we often seek release by projecting our hopes onto future achievements or acquisitions. This places an unjust demand on the future, which must now provide us with fulfillment and liberate us from our discontentment.

While many of us seek liberation externally through traveling, substances, relationships, shopping, sex, or work; few realize they are caught in an endless trap. To realize this is the starting point. It marks the beginning of an inward movement, toward the root of suffering.

To find the cure, we must face the curse.

Suffering is nature's way of initiating us into deeper wisdom.

Just as physical pain is a sign that our body needs attention, psychological suffering is an indication that our inner world is calling for attention, that we may not live in accordance with our essence.

It's a well-known fact that people sometimes experience a profound spiritual awakening after intense suffering, such as an accident or the loss of a loved one.[4] While minor suffering might drive us to alleviate only the symptoms, intense suffering can motivate us to seek the root cause of suffering, awakening us to deeper wisdom.

Ancient cultures practiced initiation rites to guide the transition to greater wisdom. Although modern society has abandoned the intentional use of rites and rituals for this purpose, our need for them has not vanished. Rather than being organized by the tribe, we are now called to initiation through suffering. In fact, suffering *is* the initiation.

An initiation is a doorway to a more harmonious way of being; a call to return home. I cannot think of a better way to beckon someone home than through suffering. It is often so uncomfortable and unbearable that it has the power to bring us to our knees, so that we no longer run away from it, but finally surrender to it and listen.

Instead of taking a pill or distracting ourselves, perhaps a more sustainable way would be to listen deeply, and see it as an invitation to (re-)assess our way of being.

When we lose touch with ourselves and others, we lose our innate joy. To compensate for this loss we seek pleasure, not realizing that it cannot fill the void.

Activities like bungee jumping and public speaking are often considered scary, but what can be truly terrifying is to be vulnerable, and share our inner most feelings.

Lao Tzu said that a man with outward courage dares to die, while a man with inward courage dare to live.[5] For many, the most frightening thing isn't death, it's truly living – that is, intimately engaging with the world from a place of truth and vulnerability; the way of the heart.

When we are fully ourselves, we are inherently joyful. Joy is not caused by things outside of ourselves, it wells up from within. This is why it is referred to as well-being. In the absence of joy, we face a huge void as we are disconnected from our source. To avoid facing this void, we often turn to pleasure, which is derived from outside of us: substances, acquisitions, entertainment and so on.

Pleasure is joy's cheap substitute. When we substitute joy with pleasure, we replace fulfillment with endless craving. As a result, we become addicted, yearning for connection without realizing that this pursuit only leads to further isolation.

The way back to joy is found by opening up, allowing ourselves to be truly vulnerable, and to connect with ourselves and others in a genuine manner. That is the way of inward courage; the way of the heart.

"The opposite of addiction is connection."
- Johann Hari[6]

**The moment you
are able to observe
your thoughts and
examine them,
you are no longer
confined by them.**

I vividly remember a very difficult time in my life many years ago. I sat in my living room one afternoon while the following thought kept repeating itself in my mind,

"Everything is meaningless."

Overwhelmed by a profound sense of nihilism and despair, I felt the weight of the world compressed within this single thought. It deprived me of my motivation and it extinguished my hope for the future. It felt very dark.

Eventually I was able to loosen up my attachment to this thought. As a result, I was able to look at the thought and examine it. Suddenly I realized how absurd the thought actually was, and how I had just blindly believed it to be true.

While I was examining the validity of the thought, another thought came to mind: "If it is true that everything is meaningless, then to think that everything is meaningless is also meaningless."

This second thought literally blew my mind. I was no longer stuck in my head. The entire weight of the initial thought disappeared. A sense of relief came to me, and I started laughing about the situation. I felt hungry and decided that cooking a meal seemed pretty meaningful. While I was cooking, an old Zen saying crossed my mind:

"No thought, no problem."

Most of our suffering originates from our story about our reality, not from reality itself.

One of the most crucial distinctions we must learn to make is the distinction between an actual situation and the narrative we construct about that situation.

For instance, losing your job may give rise to stories such as "I'm not good enough," "This should never have happened," or, "I'll never find another job."

We often mistake our thoughts for reality, perceiving them as conclusions. Conclusions are fixed and finite, but reality is ever changing and infinite. If you've lost your job, you may think it is a terrible thing, but that's a story you tell yourself. All you are certain of is that you are currently unemployed. You don't know what it means in the grand scheme of things.

We suffer not so much from what happens, but from what we tell ourselves about what happens. By learning to stay with what is without making up stories, we free ourselves from a lot of suffering. This enables us to simply ask, "What does this situation ask of me?" and to take conscious action in response. In other words, it increases our *response-ability*.

A story has a beginning and an end, a past and a future. This is where most of our suffering resides, either in memories or in an imaginative future. The only way out of a story is to wake up from it. Step out of your finite script, and wake up to the infinite Now.

To live by rationality alone is an irrational way of living.

Sometimes people are so hyper-rational that they become irrational. That doesn't mean rationality isn't useful, but that we must know its proper place.

Some spiritually minded people have an aversion against rationality. Ironically, these same people are often being misled because they naively believe everything they are told. We need critical thinking, reasoning, and logic. It's just that we also need intuition, instinct, inspiration, and sometimes a leap of faith.

Our intellect must be connected to the body. If it gets disembodied, we lose touch with reality, drifting away into concepts and theories. The intellect is very useful to conceptualize and change the world, but we need our bodily senses to actually be in touch with the world.

"The madman is not the man who has lost his reason. The madman is the man who has lost everything except his reason." - G.K. Chesterton[7]

Rationality is a great servant, but a poor chief.[8]

Ultimately, both the senses and the intellect must be transcended by, and included in, our center: the heart of awareness. Awareness enables us to harness the power of the intellect and the intelligence of the body. Pure awareness includes and transcends all of our faculties. It is neither rational nor irrational; it is *transrational*.

Judging people morally is perhaps the laziest way of the ego to feel superior.

When we label other people as bad we indirectly label ourselves as good. This is how the ego feels superior, but it is very superficial. Those who most loudly proclaim the wickedness of others are usually the most ignorant of their own shadow; condemning in others what they fail to notice in themselves.

Whenever we put a label on someone, we reduce an infinitely complex being to a simple abstraction. A moral judgment is even more simple as it classifies another human being simply as good or bad. Once we classify others as bad we think we have a legitimate reason to hate them. As hate grows, we tend to justify our own malevolent behavior toward them, still believing we are the good ones.

"The real Evil is the supposedly innocent gaze which perceives in the world nothing but Evil." – Slavoj Žižek[9]

Putting people in camps of good and bad leads to war. To see a bit of another in yourself, and to see a bit of yourself in another leads to mutual understanding, which is possibly the best antidote to war.

Does this mean we should never discern between wholesome and unwholesome? No, it means we must discern on the level of behavior, not someone's identity. By separating behavior from identity we leave room for growth, mercy, and redemption, reflecting Gandhi's timeless words, "Hate the sin and not the sinner."[10]

**Those who refuse
to take responsibility
for their pain will
always seek a scapegoat.**

When we are in the process of working on ourselves, a setback can sometimes spark anger or frustration. It is very tempting in such cases to direct our anger outward, and to blame something or someone else for our pain.

It is hard to acknowledge our own flaws, and it's even harder to make peace with them and befriend them. It's very tempting to project our anger on a scapegoat and believe that they are the source of all of our problems.

This way we don't have to deal with ourselves and we don't have to take responsibility for our own pain. Politicians, family members, minority groups, the economy; these are just a few popular scapegoats people use to escape dealing with their own pain.

Beneath much of our anger and frustration is grief. Grief for unfulfilled needs and wishes, or painful losses. Sometimes, remaining angry becomes a coping mechanism to avoid having to deal with our pain.

The problem is, no matter how many scapegoats we would be able to eliminate, our pain will still remain, and our flaws still exist. Our anger doesn't go away by getting rid of a scapegoat, it just seeks a new scapegoat.

Anger cannot embrace peace, only peace can embrace anger.

If we face the pain that lurks behind our anger, and grieve our unmet needs, we are able to come to terms with reality again, and face life head on, peacefully.

To transcend suffering we need courage to face it, compassion to embrace it, and wisdom to overcome it.

There comes a time in life when we have to face our unresolved issues. And to deal with them properly means to deal with them honestly. This requires courage. The word "courage" comes from the Latin word "cor" which means "heart." Courageous people are people with a heart; people who care deeply. As Lao Tzu said "Because of deep love, one is courageous."[11]

The more deeply we love, the more courageous we become. This is why some people only start dealing with their unresolved past after the birth of their first child. They care so much about their newborn that they are encouraged to face their own past.

Remember, what you don't transmute you transmit.

In facing ourselves, we also need compassion. We need to treat ourselves with love and care. Compassion breeds mildness, patience, and understanding. It helps us embrace our suffering to make space for healing.

And last but not least, we need wisdom. We need to develop insight into the root cause of suffering. Carl Jung believed that "The foundation of all mental illness is the unwillingness to experience legitimate suffering."[12] In other words, we're suppressing what wants to be felt. This is sometimes referred to as "ignoring the call."
So whenever you are suffering, ask yourself honestly,

"What call am I ignoring; what task am I avoiding?"

**Suffering begins
when we start
to resist what is.
It dissolves
when we allow
whatever is to be.**

Let's make a distinction between pain and suffering. Pain, whether physical or emotional, is an inevitable part of life. (Psychological) suffering, however, is a mental state that's added because of our unwillingness or inability to experience this pain. In other words, it is possible to experience pain without suffering from it.

The key to transcend suffering is equanimity. This means one doesn't react to an experience with clinging or aversion. An equanimous mind is at ease, not because it never contains a storm, but because it is never contained by it. Just like the sky can contain a storm, it is never touched by it, like a silent non-resisting witness.

A student once said to Nisargadatta Maharaj, an Indian sage, that he was continuously experiencing suffering. Nisargadatta replied, "You're not experiencing suffering. You are suffering your experiencing."[13] Resistance says to an unpleasant experience, "Go away, I don't want to deal with you!" Equanimity says, "Welcome, come in, please tell me what you want me to hear."

If we allow our experience to be as it is in each moment, we are free from suffering. This does not mean there are no longer unpleasant experiences, it means we no longer suffer from them. We simply experience them and take appropriate action in response. This takes practice. Every time we release our resistance, a little death takes place. Not the death of our pain, but the death of the part in us that resists and suffers from it.

Sincerity

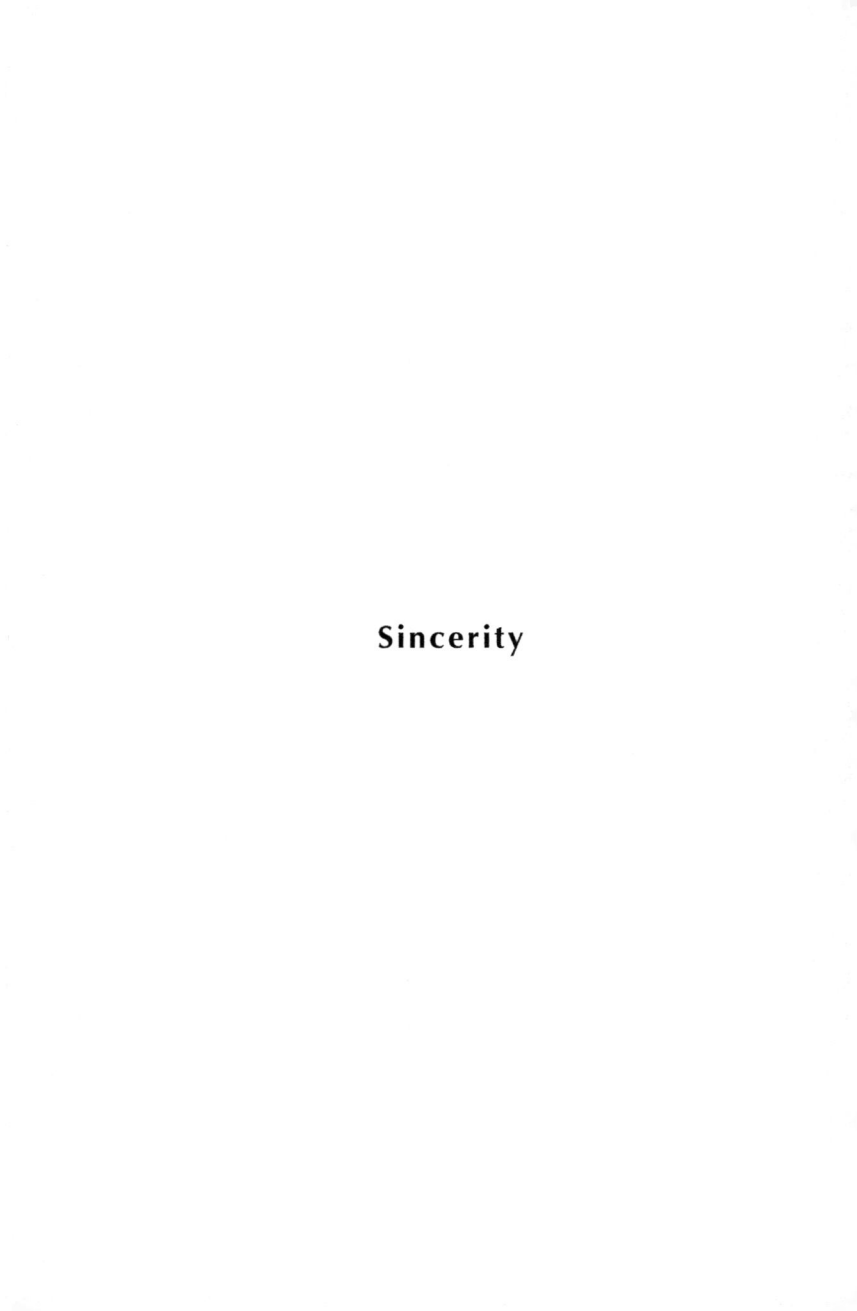

"You must go on trying to be sincere.
Each day you put on a mask,
and you must take it off little by little."

– **G.I. Gurdjieff** [14]

The point isn't to slay the dragon, it's to ride it.

Many of us learn early in life that we're not always loved for showing up as we are. As a result, we learn to hide ourselves behind masks, skillfully concealing the aspects of ourselves that are deemed unworthy.

Some of these aspects are so undesirable that we even hide them from ourselves. They make up what Carl Jung called our "shadow." The shadow refers to the parts of us that have been cast aside during the development of our personality because they didn't suit the ideal image. Think of the typical "nice guy" who suppresses his anger, or the "tough guy" who suppresses his kindness. Both are "dividuals" instead of individuals: split off, divided. Aspects we suppress often show up in unhealthy ways. They are like little eggs that grow in the dark and turn into dragons. One day they may break through the shell of our self-image and shatter it.

To become an individual, which means to be whole, we must first go where we least wish to go; inward. We must look into our darkest corners with the light of awareness and compassion. If we are courageous enough to look the dragon in the eye, we may find that it was only a neglected little angel.

Re-member your neglected "members." Don't slay your "dragons," relate to them, and learn to ride them instead. Bring all of you into harmony and the primordial force will move through you once more. This liberates you to go face the world and release your full potential.

We cannot expect
people to love us
for who we are
if we never show
our true colors.

Some people spend their lives pretending to be someone they're not, plagued by the belief that their true selves are unworthy. This leads to the creation of false personas. When people are drawn to them, they face a problem. What if someone comes too close and looks behind the mask? The fear of being exposed makes them pretend even better. As a result, the fear of not being worthy only increases.

Hiding our true colors can lead to loneliness. By hiding our true selves, no one will be able to know or see us truly. Loneliness is not about the absence of people, it's about being unable or unwilling to open up and make real contact with ourselves and others.

The more we pretend, the more we fear intimacy. Intimacy requires sincerity. It is a great practice to reveal parts of yourself to someone you can trust, until you are able to relax fully as yourself. Being yourself is a matter of relaxation; of letting go of the tension of trying to live up to an image of who you think you should be.

Be aware how many times a day you say or do things only to be seen in a certain way. Notice your body: if your words and actions are wholesome, you feel grounded. If not, you feel shaky. This doesn't mean you should throw your masks in the bin. They may have saved your life, and are still useful in many situations. Honor them, but don't identify with them. This way, you become less serious about them and more playful.

**If you don't
dare to say no,
your yes
means nothing.**

Every time we say yes while we actually mean no, we harm not only our soul, but also our relationships.

People who can't say no are called pleasers. Pleasing harms relationships because a pleaser never shows his true colors. This makes pleasers untrustworthy as people cannot know where they stand in relation to the pleaser. Compassion is selfless, but pleasing is selfish. Why? Because pleasers act with the intent to be liked, but be careful, that doesn't imply that they like you.

To become mature, we must be congruent and sincere. We must dare to be truthful in word and action. This makes us vulnerable because it may cause conflict or rejection; the pleaser's greatest fears. But if we do not have the courage to be disliked, we cannot have real intimacy.

This is not an invitation to always bluntly say what you think. Being truthful doesn't mean to always speak your mind, but rather to always mind your speech.

Beware of your motives. Sincerity has no agenda. Be dedicated to truth while also being committed to the well-being of yourself and others. Compassionate people speak sincerely, not to harm others, but to help them fly to greater heights. And to fly, people need two wings: truth and love. No one can fly with one wing only. For love without truth is deceptive, and truth without love is destructive.

Do you use spiritual teachings to heal from your wounds or hide from them?

The therapist and meditation teacher John Welwood observed that many Western people use spirituality to avoid facing their psychological wounds. He called this "spiritual bypassing,"[15] a kind of premature awakening in which people fall in love with the idea of enlightenment whilst hiding, or dissociating from, their real feelings and emotions.

This isn't sincere spirituality. We cannot grow from what we hide, we can only grow from what we bring to light. Healing isn't about becoming superhuman, it's about becoming fully human. Spiritual teachings invite us to be vulnerable, not perfect. Perfection intimidates, but vulnerability inspires. This doesn't mean we stop dealing with our flaws, but that we stop condemning them.

"We cannot change anything until we accept it.
Condemnation does not liberate, it oppresses."
— Carl Jung[16]

If we condemn ourselves, we become an enemy to ourselves. If we accept ourselves, we become a friend to ourselves. Self-acceptance can be profoundly liberating. It releases the tension between what we are and what we think we must be. The energy that is released when we stop fighting against ourselves can then be used to productively cooperate with the reality of this moment.

This moment is all there ever is. Be aware, be still, and listen. Wholesome action never arises from a place of agitation; it arises from a place of calmness.

**When we unveil
our deepest yearning
we may find not only
inspiration, but also
terror; the terror
of having to face
our deepest fears.**

Have you ever considered that what you want most deeply is also what you are most terrified of? Whether it's an intimate relationship, a business, or just being who you truly are.

Whatever it is that we yearn for, it demands us to face what stands in the way. Maybe we yearn for an intimate relationship, but we're terrified of rejection. Maybe we yearn to be our true selves, but we're terrified of social exclusion. Maybe we yearn to be an entrepreneur, but we're terrified of financial uncertainty.

As a result, some people are so scared that they'd rather bury their deepest yearning. But by doing so they also bury their *élan vital*, their very life force. Life not lived turns against itself. Self-destructiveness, hatred, and resentment are the poisonous fruits of an unfulfilled life.

"If you bring forth what is within you, what you bring forth will save you. If you do not bring forth what is within you, what you do not bring forth will ruin you."
- Gospel of Thomas[17]

To listen to the call of the heart is an act of courage, it demands our full being. It forces us to face our deepest fears. This is a noble task, but it won't be without pain.

However, there are two kinds of pain. One is the result of fleeing from your task. The other is the result of facing your task. Which one will you choose?

One of the biggest obstacles for awakening is our desire to be special.

The further we proceed on the spiritual path, the more subtle the ego becomes in its attempts to deceive us.
It may take off one jacket, but it may take on another one straight away. It craves admiration. Maybe you have quit your corporate career, and you start visiting yoga retreats. Before you know it your ego replaces its corporate jacket for a spiritual one. After a while you learn that you have to surrender your desire to be special. Now your ego may try to be recognized as special by trying to come across as someone who has no need to feel special – a subtle maneuver.

Or, you read a lot of spiritual books and then flaunt your knowledge at every occasion. You may even start looking down on those poor people who are still asleep. This is ego-glorification, not spiritual growth. Spiritual awakening isn't about becoming special or attaining something special. It's about recognizing your naked being; nothing special. As long as you try to be special, or find something special, you remain ignorant.

No one sees through the veil, but who dares to be no one?

If we are ignorant and we recognize it, we are already awakening. If we don't recognize it, we may falsely believe we are awake. Ignorance of ignorance is the most persistent form of ignorance.

"If you see the illusion you are enlightened, but if you think you are enlightened you are in the illusion."
- H.W.L. Poonja[18]

**Insincerity means
to sacrifice truthfulness
for the sake of one's ego.**

**Sincerity means to
sacrifice one's ego for
the sake of truthfulness.**

One of the first questions we have to ask ourselves if we pursue a spiritual path is, "What is my intention?"

If we explore our intentions, we will find that they are rooted in our innermost desires and values. They spring from what we worship. If we worship our ego, we will probably use spiritual insights to boost our ego. If we worship the good, we will probably use spiritual insights for the sake of helping ourselves and others live better.

Spiritual growth isn't measured by our actions but by the spirit in which they're taken. It's easy to change what we do, it's way harder to change what we worship.

In ancient Greece, when philosophy was still considered a way of life rather than merely an intellectual endeavor, there was a lot of emphasis placed on what was called "askesis," a kind of spiritual training meant to cultivate virtues such as humility, integrity, and courage.[19]

Why? Knowledge without virtue is dangerous. An evil person armed with deep truths can cause big trouble.

"It is better to will the good than to know the truth."
– Petrarch[20]

The aim of the spiritual path is not to know the truth, but to find a way to live in accordance with the truth.

It's about transformation, not just information. There is no final truth to *attain*. The point is to learn to abide in truthfulness and sincerity, to stay on the narrow way.

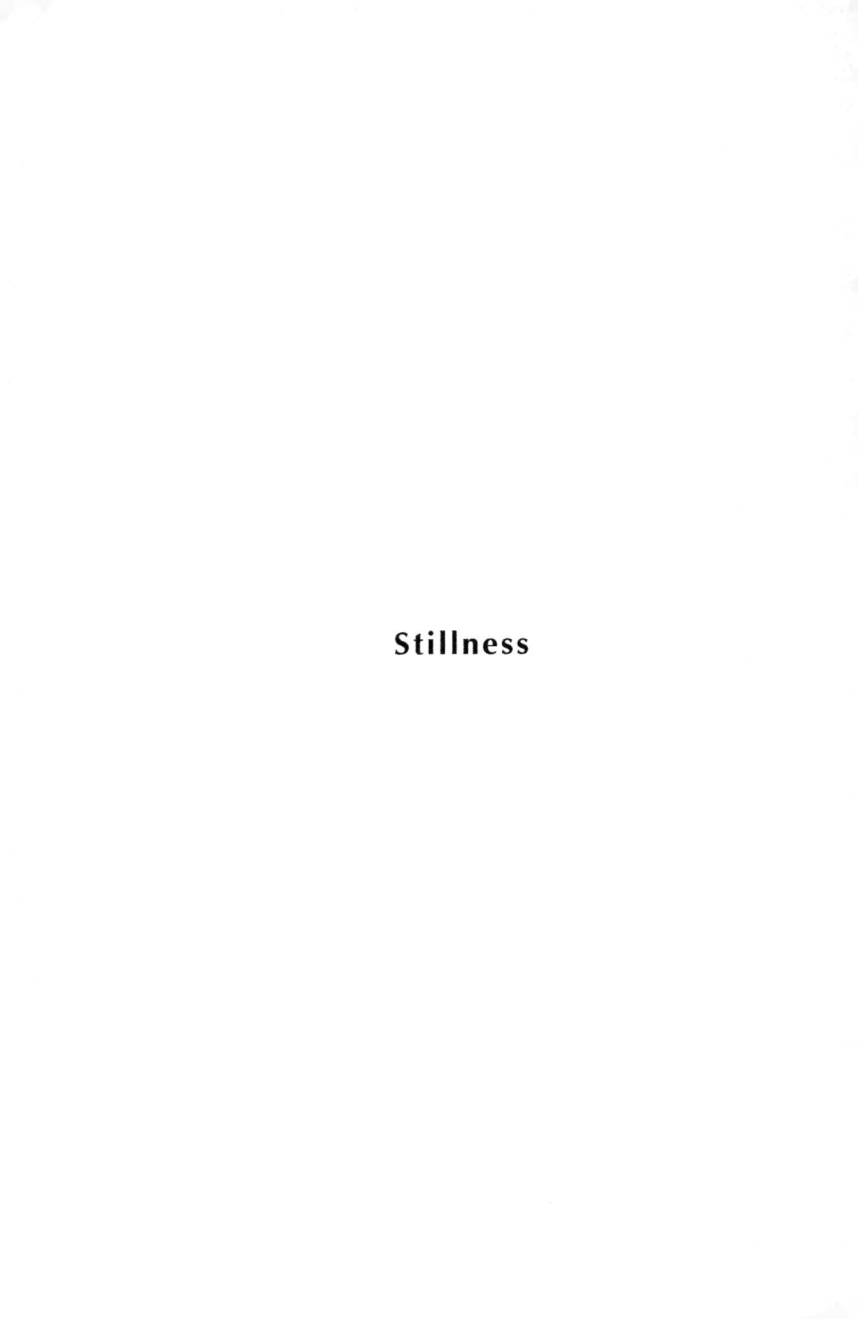

Stillness

"In each of us there is a silence, a silence as vast as the universe. We are afraid of it . . . and we long for it. When we experience that silence, we remember who we are."

— **Gunilla Norris**[21]

Silence is the absence of outer noise.

Stillness is the absence of inner noise.

In the spring of 2018, I visited the forest with my mentor to celebrate his birthday together. As he could no longer walk very well, I put him in his mobility scooter while I accompanied him by bicycle.

It was a beautiful day and my mentor was visibly enjoying the beauty of a blossoming forest in spring. While we were sitting on a little hill looking out over the landscape while enjoying the sun and the sound of the birds, he suddenly uttered the following words:

"As an individual I belong only to myself. As a human being I belong to all of humanity. As a life form, I belong to all of life. In essence, I am the essence of all that is."

It took me years to grasp what he meant by that. Now I see why these words came to him in the forest. Even though a forest is full of sounds, there is also an alive stillness that beckons us into itself. An inner quietness through which we feel deeply in touch with our essence.

The little noise in the head, the ego, with all its defense mechanisms quietens. No tree judges you if your hair looks strange, or if you don't conform to societal norms. This transcendence of ego causes a deep relaxation that expands us until we are one with our essence. Not a unique individual essence, but the one formless essence of which all of us are merely individual expressions.

"Nature is not a place to visit, it is home." - Gary Snyder[22]

Stillness is the friend of wisdom. Busyness is its enemy.

Most people don't realize how incredibly fast and noisy their modern lives have become until they disconnect from it for a while. This realization can be quite shocking. So many people are just numbing themselves in an attempt to silence their inner voice, so that they don't have to come to terms with the fact that the rat race they are in isn't leading anywhere.

So they keep running, chasing the golden carrot while the gold within gets buried deeper and deeper.

"Those who are wise won't be busy, and those who are too busy can't be wise." – Lin Yutang[23]

The wise seek solitude from time to time, not to escape the world, but to be able to live effectively in the world.

I once read an article about a very successful inventor. When asked how he became so successful, he said he spent 20 hours of his work week walking in the forest.

Stillness is the place where creativity blooms. Wise people take time to meditate, contemplate, and reflect to sharpen their perspectives. They have one foot in the world, and one foot in the woods. If they only abide in the world, they lose touch with themselves. If they only abide in the woods, they lose touch with the world.

We spend too much time figuring out how to achieve our goals and too little time figuring out whether our goals are actually worth achieving.

Whenever I visit the self-help section in a book store I am astonished by the amount of How-to-books I see on the shelves. "How to get a perfect body," "How to get rich," "How to win more clients" – each promising us to realize our dreams. We are so absorbed by our pursuits, that we often fail to reflect on the intrinsic worth of our ambitions. Sometimes our wildest ambitions are but the external manifestations of our childhood wounds.

Think of the adult who is still trying to disprove a teacher who once said, "You'll never amount to anything." Or the person who seeks fame in an attempt to satisfy his or her craving for admiration. Think of all the men who, though hailed as champions in the public eye, remain haunted by their painful childhoods – little boys aching for paternal approval they feel they never received.

"People may spend their whole lives climbing the ladder of success only to find, once they reach the top, that the ladder is leaning against the wrong wall."
- Thomas Merton[24]

We often blindly follow our drives without examining them. What drives us doesn't always serve us, and what we want is not always what we need. Therefore It's worth contemplating what motivates you. The following questions may be helpful to consider,

"Does what I am pursuing really serve me and the world around me?" "Does what I desire come from a place in me that is empty or full?" "Am I driven by lack or love?"

**Loneliness is the
pain of feeling
disconnected from
yourself and others.**

**Solitude is the joy
of feeling connected
to yourself and
the present moment.**

Imagine you are at a wonderful party with people who are dear to you, for example your friends or family. You feel a sense of belonging, connection, and joy. Imagine that everything around you suddenly fades away, as if it was all a dream. A few minutes later you are left all by yourself in a vast and empty desert.

The first thing you notice is the total absence of sounds, people, and objects. Immediately unpleasant thoughts pop up about your situation. You are strongly resisting the new situation. You miss the people, and the sense of connection and joy. You cannot accept the fact that you're suddenly all by yourself in a desert.

But there's no way out. You're stuck in the desert. After a while you surrender to the situation. Suddenly there's a second thing you notice: the presence of stillness. A slight peace, a subtle joy comes over you. You become aware of an all-encompassing presence to which you feel intimately at one with.

The first realization refers to loneliness, the pain of feeling disconnected from oneself and others. The second realization refers to solitude, the joy of feeling connected to oneself and the present moment.

Now the real question is: if you could be returned to the party, can you remain in touch with the stillness?

"A man must learn to acquire an inward desert, wherever and with whomever he is." – Meister Eckhart[25]

You can only think about what you already know, that's why fresh insights always come when you're not thinking.

In today's fast-paced digital age, we're constantly bombarded with information, making it easy to fall into the trap of overthinking. While thinking is useful, fresh insights often emerge from moments of inner calmness, not constant thinking.

For some people, the act of thinking has turned into an addiction. They are consumed by their own thoughts. They get stuck in a loop of repetition. Their thoughts are like canned food, no longer fresh. In an attempt to get unstuck they try to think harder, like a rat trying to escape the rat race by running faster.

True clarity and fresh insight comes not from endless analysis but from moments of genuine presence.

Whenever you are stuck in your head, take a step back. Engage with the world around you. Go for a walk, strike a conversation with a stranger, cook a nourishing meal, or craft something beautiful with your hands. By doing something new, spontaneous, we cannot depend on our old modes of being so we are awakened by a freshness.

Some problems in life cannot be solved on the level of thinking, they can only be solved when our thinking mind becomes still. As Albert Einstein wisely pointed out, "I think 99 times and find nothing. I stop thinking, swim in silence, and the truth comes to me."[26]

**The more mindful
we become in
our daily routines,
the more meaningful
they become.**

There's a sacredness that's concealed in ordinary reality that remains hidden until we become aware of it. It's through subtlety of awareness that reality reveals its splendor. The reason we cannot see this is that we constantly try to escape the dreadfulness of daily life. We're endlessly scrolling, consuming, chasing, and thinking. As a result, our minds are constantly agitated. We become like what we surround ourselves with.

Instead of trying to escape daily reality, what would happen if we did the exact opposite? What if we would give our full attention to our mundane daily rituals?

The way we attend to things changes how we perceive them. Our awareness has the power to harmonize reality in a way that it becomes more beautiful.

The sharper our awareness the more subtle realities we are able to perceive. Deeper meanings are revealed only when we are fully present.

So when eating, eat with your full attention. When cooking, cook with your full attention. When greeting people, greet them with your full attention. Do this until the point that your mind gets so rooted in the present moment that it becomes still. Only a still mind is able to notice the beauty that's contained in each moment. Practice this regularly and you will notice that your life becomes more harmonious, more peaceful, and more meaningful.

A busy mind cannot embrace the vast stillness within you, but the vast stillness within you can embrace a busy mind.

Beyond the realm of a quiet mind versus a busy mind, there is an all-encompassing stillness that transcends the mind altogether, and that is available right now.

To realize this eternal stillness doesn't mean we have to silence our thoughts. This is a misconception that many people have about stillness and meditation.

Stillness is already here. The thought, "I must silence my mind" is a thought that appears in the stillness of awareness. Trying to resist your thoughts produces only more thoughts. The attempt to quiet the activity of the mind is itself an activity of the mind. It comes from the mistaken perception that you are the mind, the thinker.

If it is snowing outside, no one asks, "Who is snowing?" Yet, when thoughts run through our mind, we say, "I am thinking." But are you? Who thinks? Who dreams at night? Is it you doing that, or do thoughts and dreams merely appear within you?

When I speak of stillness as the absence of inner noise, I don't mean there are no thoughts, images, or memories in your mind, but rather that there is no you that tries desperately to resist or hold on to them. The noise that is produced by the inner voice that tries to shut down the mind comes to rest once we realize we are not the mind and its activity. The vast space of awareness is untouched by the mind in the same way that the sky never gets wet, no matter how hard it rains.

The most powerful reaction is non-reaction.

The French Philosopher Blaise Pascal once wrote that "all of humanity's problems stem from man's inability to sit quietly in a room alone."[27] This statement holds deep wisdom, as finding solace in solitude is quite challenging. If we sit still long enough, we will sooner or later be confronted with the daunting depths of our own mind.

The longer we sit, the more "dragons" we encounter: temptations, painful memories, anxiety, restlessness, loneliness, and boredom. The mind will do anything to keep us from facing what lurks beneath its surface.

However, if we persist, sitting without reacting and allowing whatever shows up to come and go, we will soon learn a few profound lessons. Firstly, we will realize that true freedom emerges from non-reaction. Non-reaction liberates us from our conditioned patterns, and from the mind's relentless urge to grasp, seek, and cling.

Secondly, as we navigate through the dark and dim forest of the mind, at some point - by letting go of grasping, seeking and clinging, we move out of the forest. As we leave the forest behind, we enter a vast and immense kingdom. A paradise, right at our very center.

Though we cannot see nor touch it, it is ever present. Buried deep in the here and now. It is the eternal womb that is the source of all truth, love, and beauty. Enter it and you will remember who you are.

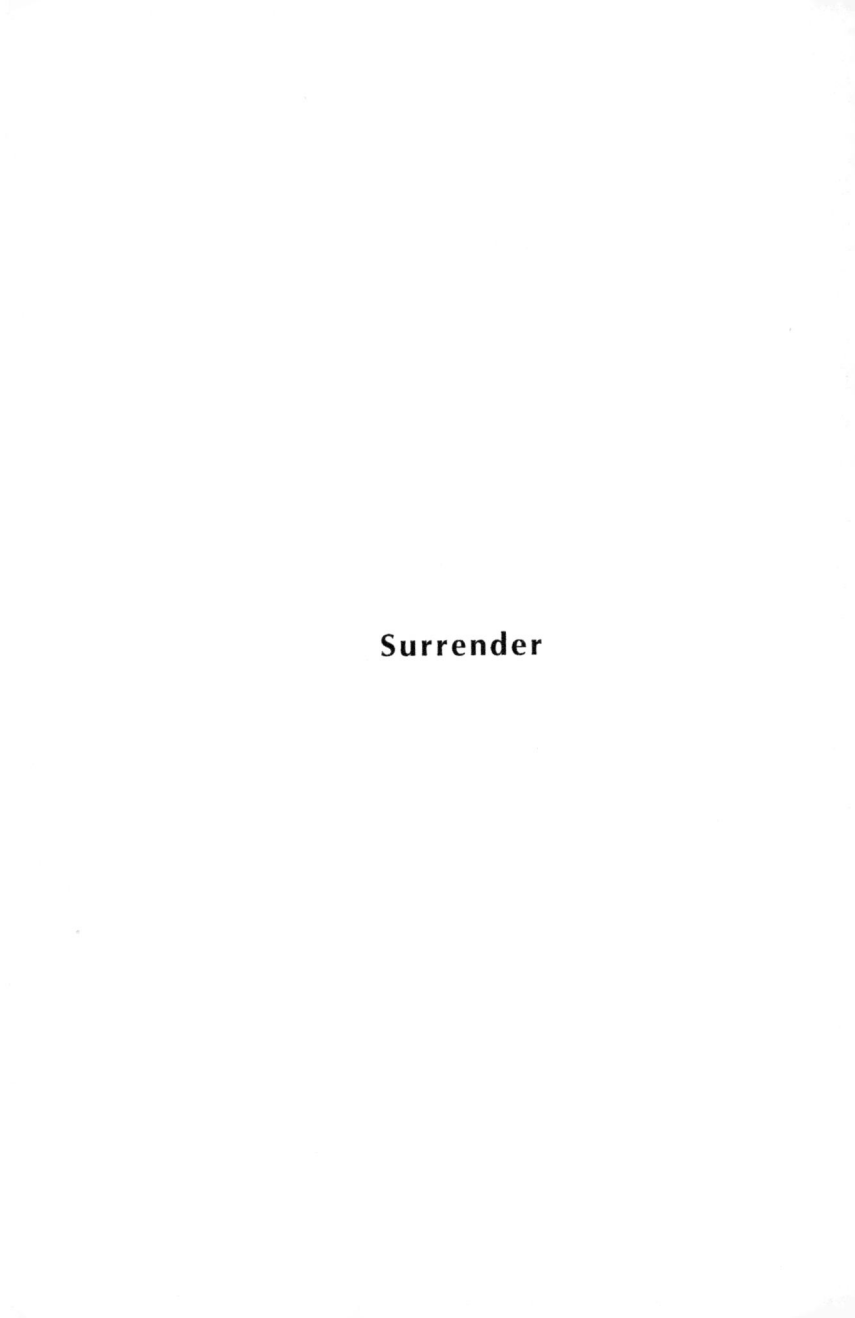

Surrender

"Peace comes not by establishing a calm outward setting so much as by inwardly surrendering to whatever the setting."

- **Hubert Van Zeller**[28]

We cannot feel the pull of our calling if we keep being pushed around by our cravings.

Imagine you find yourself craving something, whether it's a chocolate bar, alcohol, new clothes, or anything else. When you get what you want, you feel satisfied, perhaps even complete. After a while, the feeling wears off and the craving returns. Maybe even stronger. If you examine what happens, you see that you're not really attached to the thing you want, but to the feeling you get once you have it.

Craving causes a tension that we try to eliminate by satisfying it. It is a never-ending trap, arising from the illusion that we are not yet complete.

If we surrender to the feeling of incompleteness, we find that beneath it usually lies an uncomfortable feeling we want to avoid. If we welcome that feeling too and surrender to it, we liberate the life energy behind it.

Freedom from craving doesn't mean you no longer have desires. Conversely, when we're empty of craving and clinging, a different kind of desire awakens, one of a noble quality – the subtle pull of our true calling. It's the transpersonal will seeking expression through us.

This is the conscious surrender to life, the existential yes! A yes, not to our personal will, but to a higher will moving through us. Perhaps that is what a free will truly means, a will that is liberated from personal attachments, so we can freely and joyfully do what we are called to do.

The more we run away from uncomfortable experiences, the more we reinforce them.

Imagine you experience an unsettling feeling, perhaps boredom. Many instinctively resist or try to escape such a feeling, not willing to endure discomfort. Yet, in this resistance we actually strengthen it. By running away from it we give it more power and substance.

If we surrender to the feeling of boredom, and allow it its existence, we may learn that we can just face it. Next time you find yourself bored, see if you can allow the feeling. Don't resist it. Instead, go into it. Explore it. This teaches us to find comfort amid discomfort, and rest in the midst of restlessness. Instead of trying to get rid of unpleasant feelings, we learn to face them. By doing so, what seems to be a snake may turn out to be just a rope.

All experiences are transient. Once we recognize this, both clinging to pleasant experiences, and resisting unpleasant experiences come to an end. As a result, experiences start losing their power over us.

Not only are feelings and moods impermanent, but the perceptions that come with them are too. Our outlook in moments of despair differs vastly from those of delight. None of these perspectives encapsulate the truth; they are reflections of our inner state. As feelings fade, these perceptions also melt like snow under the sun.

To find inner peace, don't seek it in the ebb and flow of your experiences. Instead, look for the emptiness within all experiences, and find the hidden treasure there.

In time, peace
cannot be found.

In expectation,
it is suspended.

In surrender,
it is right here.

When I first started meditating, I thought the point of it was to reach an end-goal; the end of suffering. I thought that if I would just meditate enough hours, I would reach a state of bliss that would be permanent. I noticed that I was particularly interested in meditation when I felt stressed. I used meditation instrumentally. As if meditation was a means to get rid of negative feelings.

After a few years I started realizing that I wasn't truly meditating. Though I had learned to just sit with what is, there was still a subtle expectation, as if somewhere in time, a hidden insight or experience would reveal itself and solve all my problems; as if I was expecting to meditate my way into some heavenly state of being.

The philosopher Peter Kreeft once wrote, "We do not do good works to get into heaven. We do good works because heaven has gotten to us."[29] I tried to get into heaven by meditating as well as possible, and therefore it remained forever out of reach. I was unaware that effort and expectation suspend realization.

Years later it started dawning on me that there was nothing to gain. Meditation has no goal, it is the goal. It is an invitation to constantly surrender expectations, resistance, and preferences. Every time we surrender, we realize we are already there. Seen this way, the kingdom of heaven is not a distant goal reached somewhere in time, but an ever present reality that beckons us into itself whenever we surrender.

To modern people, liberation is seen as a triumph *of* oneself.

To ancient people, liberation was seen as a triumph *over* oneself.

For many people today, liberation is seen as freedom for oneself; being free to do and be whatever you want.

This quest for freedom often manifests as a rebellion against authoritarian regimes, rigid doctrines, familial expectations, or societal structures. Once we are free, we usually turn to more personal constraints; freedom from gender (roles), physical constraints, limiting beliefs, or even the human body; the transhumanist's dream.

There is nothing wrong with this type of autonomy as long as it is propelled by goodness, truth and beauty, and not a rebellion against them. Otherwise it may detach us from the very ground of reality itself.[30] Think of the mythic rebellion of Lucifer who refuses to bow down in front of God because he wants to be God, himself. The Ego as God, the ultimate triumph of me.

This is not what the ancient masters meant when they spoke of liberation. For them, liberation is *from* the person, not *for* the person. Liberation, not as absolute power and control, but as a total surrender of one's wish for control. It is an inner freedom, a total affirmation of ultimate reality, not a rejection, or a rebellion against it.

Perhaps the most beautiful thing about liberation as seen from this viewpoint is that it is available right now. It is the profound realization that one is already free.

Life is either a quest for liberation or an expression of it.

**You are not really
free unless you
have surrendered
the desire to be free.**

The driving force for many of our spiritual endeavors is a yearning for freedom. This may translate as a wish to escape suffering, silence our thoughts, or get rid of overwhelming emotions. This desire to be free from anything is appealing. It promises us a state of relief.

On the surface this looks great. However, an earnest seeker will find that this quest for freedom ultimately leads to a subtle form of bondage. It binds us to a perpetual state of wanting. Herein lies the paradox of the spiritual path: the more we chase inner freedom, the further it moves away.

The desire to be free from anything perpetually puts freedom at bay. If we free ourselves from one thing, something else pops up that we aren't yet free from. And so our pursuit of freedom chains us forever. Could it be that we are chasing only a superficial form of freedom? Are we perhaps running after a false idol?

My mentor once told me that absolute freedom is the surrender to the realization that it does not exist.
In other words, real freedom isn't about escaping anything but about allowing everything to be as it is. It is a profound acceptance of all that is, without resistance or the wish for it to be otherwise. True inner freedom involves letting go of the wish even for freedom itself.

The gates to Nirvana remain forever closed unless you surrender the desire to enter them.

**Wisdom begins
where certainty ends.**

How many conflicts have arisen from the pretense of knowing the truth? How much malice is born from the pretense of knowing what is right? The noise of those who shout "I know!" prevents us from hearing the wisdom that's contained in the words "I don't know."

Socrates was considered the wisest man alive by the Oracle of Delphi. Why? Because he was the only one who knew that he knew nothing. Not-knowing is the foundation of wisdom. It takes a lot of insight to realize how much we assume we know without really knowing. No scientist knows what matter, energy, or even an atom is. They may have concepts of it, but that is an idea in their mind, the reality remains a mystery.

If we think we know reality when in fact we only know words and concepts, we will not realize our ignorance, and we will lose our sense of awe and wonder.

Our knowledge fabricates stories about reality. That's why Lao Tzu said, "Not-knowing is true knowledge."[31] To see what is going on we must drop the story and listen. To listen means to be in a state of emptiness; of not knowing. Not knowing gives rise to awareness. It creates a space that allows us to be receptive to what is going on, instead of projecting our preconceived notions onto the situation.

Essentially, not knowing is a way of being. It requires a kind of forgetting. That doesn't mean forgetting *what* we know, it means forgetting *that* we know.

**In acknowledging
our ignorance,
we invite wonder
back into our lives.**

The first time we inhale the fragrance of a rose is like being touched by wonder. The second time, the mind immediately says "That's a rose!" Instead of a magical experience, it triggers a memory. By the time we are grown up, we have memorized and labeled everything that surrounds us. The miraculous world we inhabited as children has been left behind, and what remains is a world that's fully labeled and memorized.

In labeling everything, we become spellbound by concepts. This fixation on concepts disconnects us from the immediacy of experience. We perceive reality through a filter of mental images. We no longer see reality as it is, we see the labels and images that we project on it. We are lost in the map, unable to find the territory.

Spiritual growth requires a kind of unseeing before we can see clearly. It invites us to let go of preconceptions and mental projections by cultivating awareness, receptivity and openness; a so called "beginner's mind."

In doing so, we learn to perceive things as they are, beyond the images we have projected on them. As we inhale the scent of a flower, hear the wind in the trees, or watch the night sky, we are enthralled by the living mystery, as if perceiving it for the very first time again.

"If the doors of perception were cleansed then everything would appear to man as it is, Infinite."
- William Blake[32]

A mind shaped by a single perspective is like an eye that sees but one color.

If we are interested in awakening, we must be careful not to get attached to our viewpoints of reality. My mentor used to say, "The invitation is to open yourself up to let go of an insight, no matter how beautiful it is, so that ever more beautiful insights can be welcomed."

No viewpoint captures reality fully, no theory can explain everything. Ultimate reality transcends any description, conception, or theory of it. At their best, concepts can point to it, but they are not it. As Buddhists say, "The finger pointing to the moon is not the moon."

Fanaticism, whether in religion, spirituality, or science, is to mistake the finger for the moon. By mistaking the pointer for the truth, we claim to possess the truth. As a result, we tend to criticize or even fight other fingers.

Sometimes, our very image of what we seek prevents us from seeing it. I remember one day in my office I couldn't find a stapler even though it was right in front of me. The reason I failed to see it is that the stapler I had in mind was different from the one on my desk.

To wake up, we have to realize that every notion, every word, every description ultimately becomes an obstacle on the path. Dare to be a beginner every single day; show up empty-minded. Only then can the ineffable truths that the spiritual traditions point to start unveiling themselves in the immediacy of your experience.

"The Tao that can be told is not the eternal Tao."
— Lao Tzu[33]

The more we try to grasp the essence of life, the more it slips out of our hands.

There are two ways of approaching reality. One is to seek to solve the mystery of existence, to have the final answer. The other is to open oneself up to ever greater mysteries; to expand one's capacity to be in awe.

One is the way of increasing one's knowledge; the way of grasping. The other is the way of expanding one's capacity for unknowing; the way of openness.

The way of grasping is pointed toward satisfaction. It's finite. It lives by the assumption that somewhere in time we will have all information. It's driven by the desire for closure. It's the urge for certainty masked as curiosity.

The way of openness is oriented toward emptying oneself. It's open, receptive, and free. It's inspired by wonder, not wanting. Wanting wants to possess. It is the grasping hand that seeks something to hold on to. Wonder has no wants. Its palms are open.

Ask yourself, what is there to grasp anyway? Everything in life constantly changes. Each instant is brand new. What is there to hold on to? What certainty?

Let go, open up, and listen. Do you hear the birds? Do you feel the sun on your face?

"The bird of paradise lands only on the hand that does not grasp." – Zen proverb[34]

No amount of effort can bring about an awakening.

In our quest for awakening, there comes a moment where we must realize that spiritual awakening doesn't occur by effort or striving. We may need discipline to train our mind, but that is no guarantee for insight.

Awakening is not the result of adding more content to our mind, or of achieving extraordinary skills. It isn't a badge of honor. It is simply a realization.

What the seeker looks for is beyond striving, beyond effort, and even beyond comprehension. Yet all of this may be necessary to get us to a very crucial realization. Every scripture we've absorbed, every moment of introspection and meditation, draws us to one pivotal point; the point where the ego faces its own limitations. It has to confess: enlightenment is beyond my grasp.

And in that surrender, the light of awareness shines forth. As we release our burdens, we are bathed in divine light. In simply being, we recognize our true Self.

The irony is: the ego needed a carrot to chase, otherwise it would've never started the journey. Enlightenment is ego's ultimate carrot: the promise of becoming Godlike.

However, the poor ego didn't realize it had to face its own disappearance in the process. We don't come to the Divine by striving to reach all the way up to heaven. Instead, the Divine reaches down to us when we lower our guards in humility and surrender.

Shift

"You are awareness disguised as a person."

- **Eckhart Tolle**[35]

Occasionally we outgrow an old way of being before a new one has emerged.

Sometimes, as we evolve, we find ourselves in a liminal space—a threshold where our familiar way of being is dissolving, yet the new one hasn't yet been born.

We may experience a declining interest in the life we've always known. The games that once engaged us lose their appeal. This transition isn't merely superficial—it's a profound realignment of our core values. What we held dear before may have lost its significance.

Such shifts can leave us feeling lost, like the very ground beneath us is falling away. In such moments, the instinct might be to act immediately, to regain control. However, this is not a period to rush key decisions. It's a time for patience and reflection. It can be helpful to seek guidance from mentors or teachers. These periods also ask of us to be deeply honest with ourselves.

Transformation requires a confrontation with the unknown. The known is inherently familiar, and the idea of leaving it behind can be terrifying.

We often weigh the risks of taking a new path, but we seldom consider the risks of remaining on a path we've naturally outgrown. Which risk will you choose?

Transformation demands sacrifice. Like gold refined in fire, it's in the heat of transformation that the layers of falsehood are eradicated, leaving behind a more genuine version of ourselves.

Sometimes, when we become a friend to ourselves, we become a stranger to others.

One of the ways to measure spiritual growth is by the degree to which we befriend ourselves. Being a friend to ourselves means treating ourselves with respect and to hold ourselves in high esteem, regardless of our flaws. If loving others means willing the best for them, loving ourselves means wanting the best for ourselves too.

As we grow spiritually, truth begins to outweigh personal gain. Consequently, our attachment to egoic outcomes diminishes. As the ego loses its grip over us, its needs lose their potency. We no longer depend on others to amplify our sense of self, or to feel good about ourselves. When we grant ourselves permission to be who we are we no longer need outward permission.

As a result, some relationships deepen and become more sincere, while others dissolve. Some people may be delighted by the newfound truthfulness while others may be unsettled by it. Certain friendships may fall away like leaves from a tree, making room for more genuine connections to blossom.

This process takes time, Sometimes relationships might seemingly dissolve at first, only to re-emerge later in a new form. Be patient and allow life to unfold naturally as you dedicate yourself to a more genuine way of being.

Committing to truth means dedicating yourself to a way of being, not to a predetermined outcome.

**To be yourself is
to be empty of self.**

I can recall the exact moment when I first realized I wasn't who I thought I was. It was during a deep meditation session in my bedroom, having sat there immersed in deep silence for more than an hour.

A little further down my street, construction workers were busy renovating a set of houses. At some point, a heavy object fell on the street, probably a steel pipe. The sound was so loud that it made the entire street's windows tremble, with the reverberation reaching all the way up to my bedroom.

At that instant, my body felt like a gong that had been struck. There was a strong ripple of vibrations throughout my body. Normally, I would've been shocked by such a sudden noise, tensing up. But that day was different. Even though I noticed a slight tendency of my body to tense up, I could merely witness it happening. It was not me tensing up, it was merely a pattern of reactivity that got triggered in my body.

I simply noticed the vibrations, and the echo of the noise passing through me and then dissipating, leaving no trace of fear or shock. It was as though there was no 'me' to react to the noise, only pure awareness witnessing the event happening.

It was a defining moment for me - the "me" I thought I was, was only an instinctual reaction. I realized that awareness is not in my body; my body is in awareness.

The point of spirituality is not to escape reality, but to wake up to it.

Spiritual people are sometimes viewed as people who try to escape reality and live in some kind of Neverland. Neverland represents eternal childhood. People who are drawn to it usually have difficulties taking responsibility. They long for some unattainable dream world without ever committing to something real, like a relationship, or a job. This way, spirituality becomes a form of escapism, driven by a secret wish to return to the mother womb.[36]

This is not what sincere spirituality is about. Neverland isn't Nirvana. One is a fantasy world, a dream. The other is a realization of the truth within, an awakening.

In the Zen tradition they speak of three phases in awakening. First you're normal like everyone else. Then you begin to think that everyone is crazy, while everyone else thinks you are crazy. Finally, you've become normal once again. This last phase is key. People often speak of awakening as if they finally see how fake the world is. They distance themselves from "the Matrix" and everyone still in it. They may even start to feel superior. This disintegrative experience is only the beginning. The real awakening comes with humility and is all inclusive.

Eventually, the point is to come to terms with life in a renewed way. A unifying resonance with all of reality, not just the parts you like. A level of intimacy that one can only attain by being childlike, but never childish.

"Enlightenment is just intimacy with all things."
— Dogen[37]

**A name refers to
a person, a form.
"I" refers to our
formless essence.**

What is a person? The word "person" is derived from the Latin "per sonare" which means "to sound through." In ancient Rome, the masks actors used in the theatres to play certain roles were called personas; wooden masks where the voice of the actor "sounded through."

From a spiritual perspective, the person is the apparent self. It is the form people see when they look at you. It is a mask in the sense that it only appears to be you. On a conventional level it is important to be able to identify someone. That's why names are helpful. And with these names come all sorts of traits that describe someone's personality. But is that really what you are?

From a spiritual perspective, the word "I" doesn't refer to a person. "I" refers to something more fundamental. The "I" is the impersonal, formless awareness that we are beneath the appearance.[38] Although each person is different, presence is not. As Rumi beautifully put it, *"The lamps are different but the light is the same."*[39]

Spiritual awakening is often expressed as "dying before you die." Who dies? The person. Awakening is the recognition that you are awareness itself, not a unique person. This doesn't mean you deny your personality, or try to get rid of it. It simply means you wake up from the illusion of being your personality and recognize yourself as awareness. As if you wake up from a dream at night and recognize you were not the character in your dream; you are the awareness to which it appeared.

It is the ego itself that denies or opposes the ego.

The ego is a kind of image we hold of ourselves. It's a picture painted not only in our own minds but also in the minds of others, which we try to maintain and develop over time. When this image is threatened, it can feel like a personal attack. This is called ego-identification.

Once we understand we are not this ego, but rather that the ego is a kind of illusory self-concept, we risk perceiving the ego as an adversary that must be eradicated. This attitude may lead to opposition or denial of the ego.

Ironically, the effort to deny the ego is, in itself, an act of the ego—attempting to project a new image, this time of someone devoid of ego.

Furthermore, opposing the ego suggests that we believe the ego is an enemy. The ego is not an enemy; it is only a survival reflex born from the fear of being insignificant; of being no one. It seeks its own recognition.

If we recognize ourselves simply as "awareness", the need for external validation diminishes. Awareness is already aware of being aware. There's nothing to proof and there's no-one to be. This doesn't imply the immediate absence of our egoic tendencies. They can still be triggered in certain situation. Although the ego is ultimately an illusion, it takes time before deeply ingrained patterns of reactivity lose their power.

The great irony of spiritual seeking is that we tend to search everywhere for ourselves except right here.

Many spiritual seekers hop from spiritual event to spiritual event, from book to book, and from one teaching to another. Chasing enlightenment. Before we know it, we have turned our material consumerism into spiritual consumerism. Instead of a thirst for material objects, we now have a thirst for spiritual experiences.

In many spiritual traditions, an experience is also considered an object: a sense object. An object refers to that which appears in awareness. This could be anything from physical objects to sounds, smells, tastes, thoughts, feelings, sensations, memories, images and so on. In other words, everything that comes into awareness.

If awakening is considered to be permanent, it cannot be an experience for experiences are impermanent by nature. If what I truly am is ever present, I cannot be an object, because objects appear and disappear, this is the law of nature. Everything that arises passes away sooner or later, while the "I" remains. Then what is this "I"?

The reason so many people keep searching for themselves is that they expect to find something. In doing so, they ignore the most obvious. The essential "I" is the empty space of awareness. It is the one and only no-thing in which all things appear and disappear.

The essential "I" cannot be found in space and time for space and time appear in it. It is like daylight, it cannot be seen, but through it everything else can be seen.

**To seek is to reject
the here and now.
To see is to reject
the search.**

When we wake up, a paradigm shift occurs. I was never a person within whom awareness appears; rather I am awareness that only appears to be a person. When this is recognized, the search for ourselves comes to an end, not because we finally discovered the unique person we are, but because we see what is behind this illusion.

One of the most ancient spiritual traditions from India is called Vedanta. The word "Vedanta" is derived from two Sanskrit words: "veda" which means "knowledge," and "anta" which means "end." Vedanta refers to the knowledge at the end of the Vedas, the ancient scriptures from India. But Vedanta also has a deeper, more profound, meaning. It refers to the knowledge that ends the search for self-knowledge.

What is this knowledge? As long as we search, we are caught in the notion that something essential is lacking. As seekers we subtly dismiss what is, and seek what is not. Seeking implies that we know what we are looking for. However, the self that we seek cannot be found. We cannot grasp it, because it is that which is aware of grasping. We cannot perceive it, because it is that which is aware of perceiving. In fact there is not even an it. If we think there is an it we start seeking again. There is nothing to be found.

You are nothing in the sense that you are *no-thing*. You are nobody in the sense that you are *no-body*. Yet you are. To see this entails the end of the search.

**You cannot know
what you are.
You can only know
that you are.**

Imagine yourself in a perfect sensory deprivation tank.
You can no longer see, hear, smell, taste, or touch.
Now let's imagine you also lose access to your mind;
thoughts, memories, images, and even language.

What remains? Without your bodily senses, there is no sense of space, only here. Without your mind, there is no sense of time, only now.

Some may argue that there is now an absence of consciousness. However, while the senses depend on consciousness to function, consciousness can function without the senses. Similarly, objects need space, but space doesn't need objects. In other words, consciousness is primary.

If you no longer have any sense of what you are, where you are, or even when you are; the only thing left is the sense *that* you are. Not you as a person, or even an entity. No, what remains is the knowing without anything to know. The witnessing without anything to witness.

If all contents of consciousness are absent, and if even absence is absent, what is left is pure presence.

This presence has no age, no color, no gender, no shape, and no limitation. It is infinite, whole, fulfilled.
It is our essence that we share with all beings. It is the essential "I" of which all the great mystics speak.

Simplicity

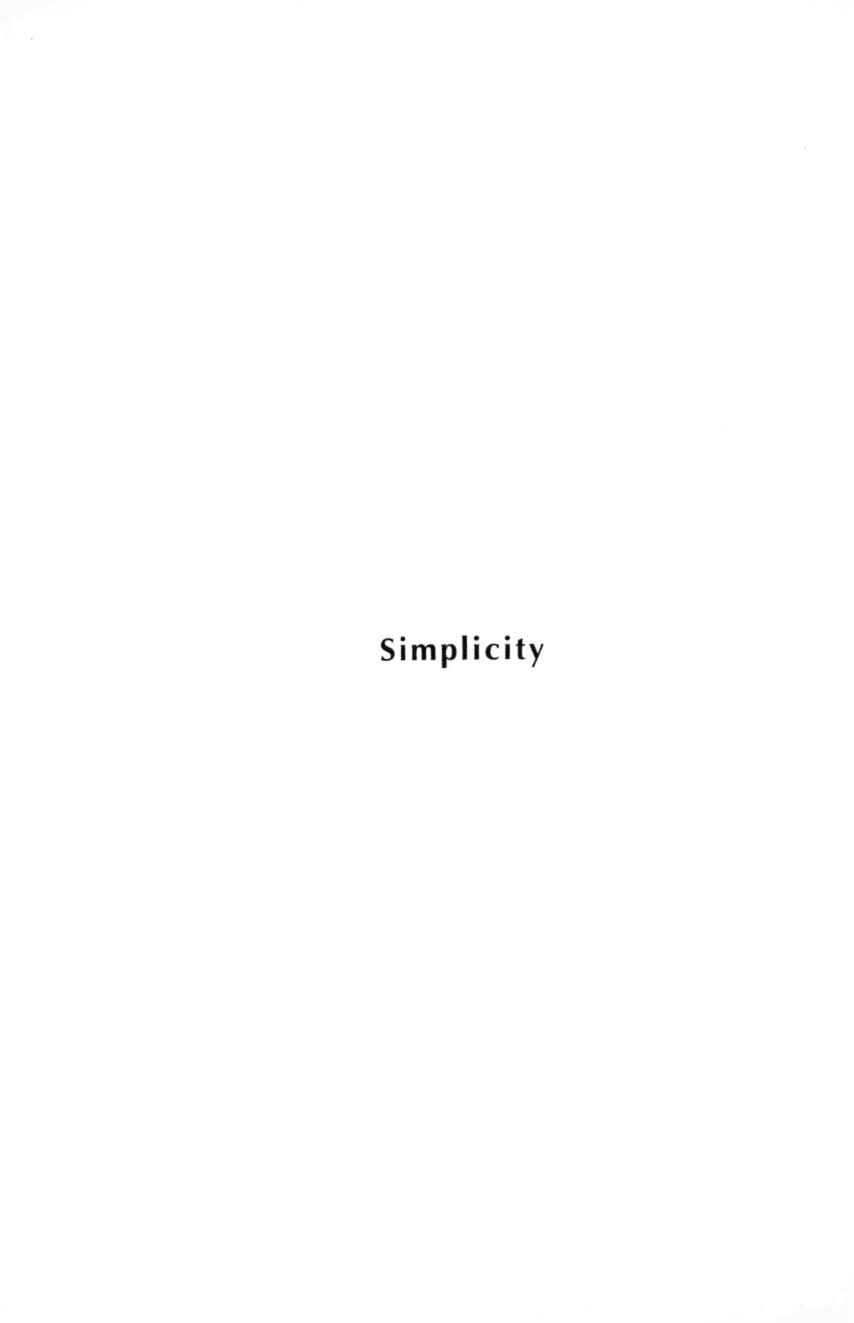

"The wisdom of life consists in the elimination of non-essentials."

- **Lin Yutang**[40]

**To know where
you must go,
ask your heart.
To figure out
how to get there,
use your head.**

To know where we must go, we need to get in touch with our intuition We need to be able to listen to the silent whispers within; this is the domain of the heart.

The heart knows not of how. It doesn't comprehend strategies, plans, and smart goals. Its realm is the call of the soul - a pull toward hidden horizons, a longing for adventure. The heart understands, but not in the way the head does. The heart knows by loving for love is its own kind of understanding.

How is a question for the head. The head knows nothing of hidden horizons. It knows not of longing. Yet, it excels in strategies and tactics to reach visible goals.

The heart and the head are companions, like two friends who embark on a journey together. They are like Frodo and Sam in the Lord of the Rings. Each plays his part; one cannot travel far without the other.

One feels the pull to go on a journey. It catches a glimpse of the possibilities that lie beyond the horizon. It dreams of hidden lands. The other one identifies the obstacles on the path and invents practical means to overcome them.

Together, they form a formidable duo as the heart sets the direction while the head navigates the journey.

Most people don't actualize their potential because they don't want to restrain themselves.

In a society that promotes instant gratification, indulgence, and boundlessness, it takes a lot of self-restraint to be able to live a fulfilling life.

The ancient wisdom of the I Ching warns us that a lack of restrictions brings misfortune.[41] Unlimited possibilities easily cause distraction, indulgence, and inertia, which in turn weakens our sense of purpose.

Recognizing the value of self-restraint is essential to a fulfilling life. Much like a game cannot be played without rules, an individual cannot flourish without limitation. Self-restraint, when exercised as a conscious choice, enables us to maintain our focus on the highest good, fostering a life of meaning and purpose. These restraints are not chains that confine us, but rather, they help us cultivate discipline and focus; they orient us.

The allure of infinite possibilities must be seen for what it is: deceptive. It is by saying no to things that distract us, that we are able to realize our potential.

To live well, we must identify what is truly important, and bring our lives in alignment with it. In other words, we must organize our lives in such a way that we are able to serve that which matters most, whatever that is.

The more we are able to withstand the temptations that seduce our mind and body, the more we are capable of following the way of the heart.

Saying yes to what matters is easy. Saying no to what doesn't matter is much harder.

Our ability to bring our lives into alignment with what is most essential depends on our ability to say no to what is not essential. The world constantly begs for our attention, and if we don't learn to use our attention properly, we will fragment our attention and lose focus.

How often do we do things out of politeness, fear of missing out, or simply because we are afraid to say no? How often do we do things on auto-pilot, without much attention?

A life that is aligned with our values is built on good decisions. Every decision is by definition a sacrifice. Every yes we give to one option is a no to many others. So the question is not, "Are you willing to say yes to those few things?" The question is, "Are you willing to say no to all those other things?"

It has been said that it's easy to make life complicated, but very hard to keep it simple. The most important thing is to discover what is most important. The second most important thing is to organize ourselves in such a way that we are aligned with what is most important.

Many of us are willing to rise, but only few of us are willing to shed the weights that keep us on the ground. Many people dare to say yes. Only a few dare to say no.

"To work in the world is hard, to refrain from all unnecessary work is even harder."
— Nisargadatta Maharaj[42]

**Many people want
to have a good life,
but only a few
people want to learn
the art of living.**

Many of us speak of life as if it is something we possess. We say, "I have a life." We also speak of ourselves in terms of what we have; our job, status, personality, beliefs, possessions, and so on. This creates the belief that our identity is nested in what we have. Erich Fromm called this "the having mode" of existence.[43] Nesting our identity in what we have creates a fragile sense of self that is constantly at risk. We will continually be afraid, either of not getting what we want, or of losing what we have. A house built on sand.

"If I am what I have and if what I have is lost, who then am I? Nobody but a defeated, deflated, pathetic testimony to a wrong way of living." - Erich Fromm[44]

If we are mainly oriented toward having, we become preoccupied with results and outcomes. This can lead to expedience, the worshipping of ends over means. The result is a life of dissonance, always swinging between satisfaction and dissatisfaction.

If we explore life, we find that everything depends on everything else. Nothing exists on its own. To exist means to co-exist. My mentor used to say, "You can only exist because the whole universe exists." Once we see this, self-centeredness makes room for "whole-centeredness." This orients us properly to learn the art of living; to live in accordance with the whole. So instead of asking, "How can I obtain a good life?" Maybe a better question is, "How can I learn the art of living?"

The answer to the question about the meaning of your life is to live in such a way that the question becomes irrelevant.

Freud once pointed out that "the moment a man questions the meaning and value of life, he is sick."[45] To question life's value is usually a sign of being isolated, disconnected, or alienated. But to think about the meaning of our life abstractly is to miss the mark. We don't need a beautifully articulated answer that captures our life's meaning. There is no answer, and most definitely not on the cognitive level. What we really yearn for is the vital sense of being fully alive.

This doesn't mean we should merely distract ourselves from the question by chasing hedonistic desires. It means that we should live in such a way that the question of meaning genuinely stops bugging us.

If we expect to find some great meaning in the future, we may forever be chasing shadows. The here and now is filled with wonder and awe, but it doesn't come to us by abstract contemplation, it comes to us by opening up and actively engaging with it. The recognition that life is an endless adventure that continues to unfold itself in the here and now puts us in the right mindset to experience the thrill of being alive.

We tend to think that the value of life is determined by the actualization of our potential, the people we love, and the possessions we acquire. But what truly enhances our lives is our ability to connect, open up and be truly present with all of that.

In our endless pursuit of more, better, and faster, we have forgotten the good.

There's a reason why the Greek philosophers promoted the good life, and not the maximized life. Modern people have forgotten about this.

Many of us have grown up in a world that has broken with almost every wisdom tradition. Especially in the Western World, we have come to believe that life is just a random event, and the goal is just to chase whatever we desire.

The result is a society that is completely utilized for this purpose; a colossal production/consumption machine.

We all work as hard as we can to make as much money as possible so that we can consume as much as we want. Many have called it the pursuit of happiness. But does this pursuit really make us happy?

It doesn't. It makes us miserable instead. Everyone is craving what everyone else has, leading to endless comparison and competition and complete inner exhaustion and depletion. The consequences of this way of living have been exhausting the entire planet.

Maybe we have to remember something the wisdom keepers of the world have always known. It sounds like a radical idea to young people: the idea of Enough. A good life isn't about having everything you desire. A good life is about knowing the difference between too little and too much.

Cheerfulness belongs to the grateful. Gratefulness belongs to the humble.

During the summer of 2019, while volunteering at a meditation center in Belgium, I learned a great lesson.

As I was in the kitchen preparing lunch for the teachers, the cheerful chirping of birds and the sunlight outside in the garden created a serene backdrop. Another volunteer was peeling potatoes beside me, and the greengrocer entered the kitchen, whistling, with fresh vegetables. As I finished preparing lunch, I went to the teacher's facility to bring the food. On my way there, I passed through an old barn where another volunteer was hanging freshly washed towels on a clothesline.

Right there, amid the fresh towels and the old wood, I was suddenly struck by a profound sense of joy and gratefulness, as if everything was in perfect harmony. At that moment, a sentence I once heard in an online lecture came to mind, "Modern men don't see God because they don't look low enough."[46]

It made me realize that not so much is needed for happiness: a useful task to be engaged in, a sense of community, a few companions, a quiet mind, and a little humility. I had often looked for happiness in the peaks of achievement, acquisition, and self-gratification.

That day was a powerful reminder to me that happiness can be found in the humblest of places, that the sacred is to be found in the midst of the mundane. I realized that cheerfulness was a matter of *self-forgetfulness*.

Serenity

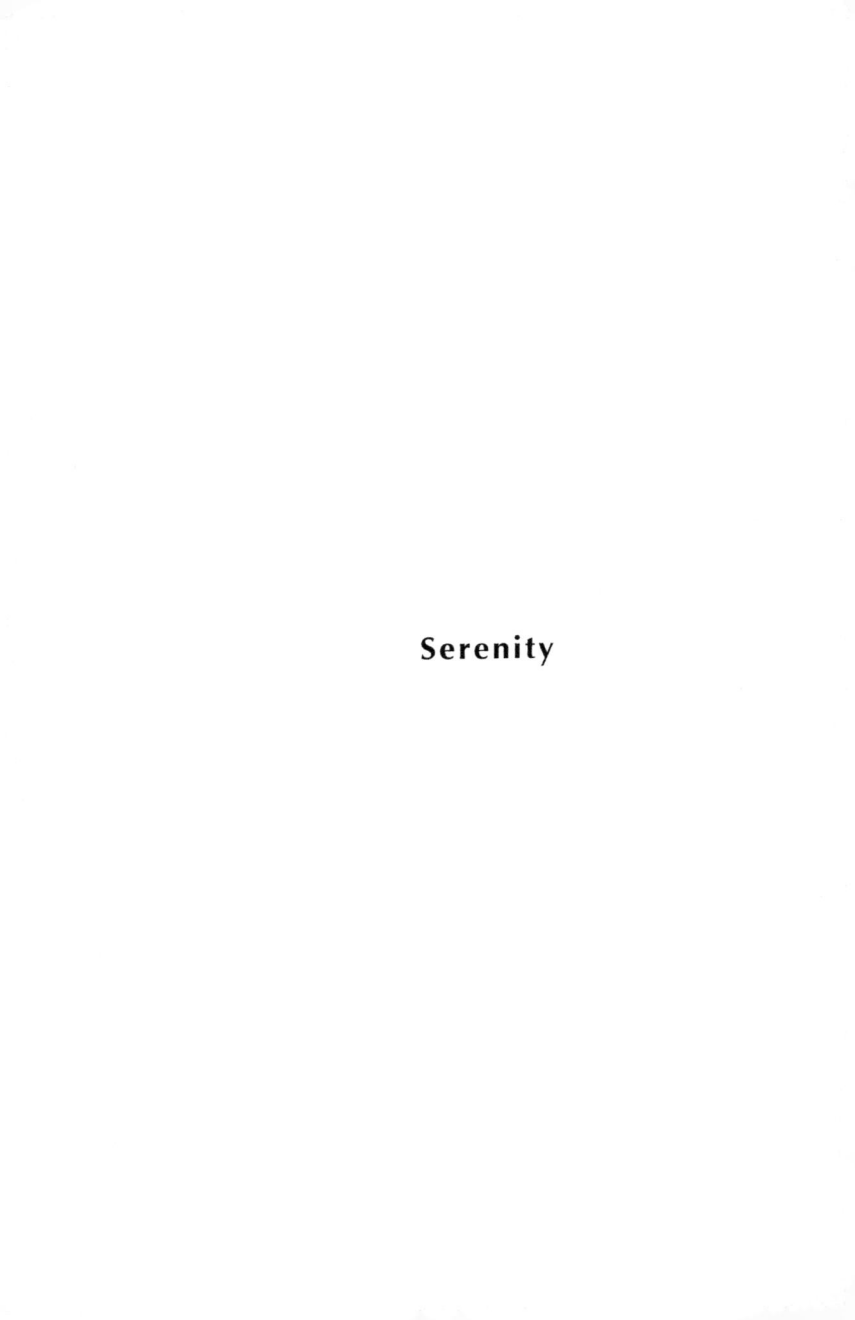

"The root of all desires is the one desire: to come home, to be at peace."

— **Jean Klein**[47]

Everything comes and goes except the Now. Be at peace with the Now and you'll be at peace with yourself.

The now has always been and will always be. Prior to the Big Bang it was already now, and long after our universe has vanished it will still be now. Now transcends time.

But what is this Now? You cannot point to it and say "there it is." It is everywhere and nowhere at the same time. It is not a point in time. It is like an empty space yet it is empty of space. It has no existence in the sense that it has no form or shape. It is no-thing. Yet this no-thing contains everything, it is the origin of the universe, prior to space and time. Everything that is and will ever be is contained within this infinite Now.

At the deepest level, I and this Now are one. Before I am a person, before I am anything, I simply am. This *I am-ness* is our essence. Although it appears as if there are many beings on this earth, many separate I's, in reality there's only one presence, one "beingness", one *Now*.

Although there are innumerable eyes in the world, if I look into a pair of eyes, I realize that the I at which I am looking and the I from which I am looking is one I.

To catch a glimpse of this is to touch eternity. To realize this fully is to inhabit the eternal Now.

"If we take eternity to mean not infinite temporal duration but timelessness, then eternal life belongs to those who live in the present." – *Ludwig Wittgenstein*[48]

The rat race stems from the illusion that time is a resource that must be utilized maximally.

In ancient times there were several ways to think of time. The Greeks had Chronos and Kairos: chronological time versus timing, or the right moment.

In other cultures there was something like do-time and be-time. The first was symbolized by the sun, the second by the moon. Why? When the sun was out, people worked to get things done: hunting, gathering and so on.

Once the sun had set, not much could be done anymore. Instead of working, people made a fire and sat around it. This was the kind of time that was symbolized by the moon. It didn't have a utilitarian purpose in the sense that nothing needed to be done, but it did have a lot of meaning. People sang, danced, and shared stories. This was the time for connection, belonging, and play. This was the time to just be.

This is exactly the kind of "time" we are losing in the world, due to our over-emphasis on doing; on utilization and exploitation. We have turned time into a resource that we must utilize maximally to get ahead. Our lives have become a massive to-do list.

Because of this, we're all running around, hurrying up, constantly afraid that we are losing time. For that reason, many of us miss the infinite richness of this moment right here. We miss it, simply because we believe that we are running out of time. And that is precisely why we are missing out on life.

At some point you may discover that nothing in this world can bring lasting peace. This fact will let you down before it sets you free.

At some point, during our search for peace and serenity, we may realize that no external sources, circumstances, or conditions can bring about lasting peace. Fame, wealth, relationships, activities, success; no matter how appealing it all may seem, none of it can bring about lasting peace.

The realization that nothing in the outside world can bring about lasting peace puts an end to the entire pursuit. There is nowhere left to go. All the illusions have vanished, and we may feel defeated, or even depressed. Especially if we have put a lot of effort in the pursuit.

When we acknowledge and accept this realization fully, something interesting happens. It may open us up to a new perspective. Nothing in this world can fulfill the impossible task of bringing us peace; what a relief! We have just liberated the world from the unbearable burden that we placed on it. Now the world is free to be as it is.

How about the peace we were longing for? If we realize that nothing outside of us can bring us peace, we will lose our motivation. We give up. At some point, we may even question the seeker in us. What is actually propelling us to seek? Who is the one that is seeking?

"To seek is to suffer. To seek nothing is bliss."
— Bodhidharma[49]

Inner peace is not a getting rid of anything but a coming to terms with everything.

When we begin the spiritual journey to inner peace, it sometimes occurs that we think the goal is to feel at peace all the time. Although this is true at some level, it is important that it is properly understood. It is often interpreted as if we should always feel positive, but this view is problematic.

For example, if a relationship comes to an end, it is normal to feel grief. If we think 'I should not feel grief because it is negative' we set up an inner conflict. Grief is a natural sensation that arises from time to time, and if we reject it, we create inner resistance. If we can allow this grief by surrendering our resistance to it, we will find that peace can exist, even in the midst of grief.

As long as we believe there are positive and negative emotions, we maintain a split in ourselves in which we welcome one half of life while rejecting the other half.

The Buddha saw attachment as the root cause of suffering. If we are attached to certain ideas, feelings, or ways of being and they are threatened, we suffer. The practice of non-attachment is a wonderful invitation to constantly surrender to whatever arises in this moment, without labeling it good or bad.

Inner peace does not depend on positive feelings or emotions, it is independent of any feeling or emotion.

**We do not find
inner peace.
The impulse to
seek it simply
vanishes and
we realize our
innate peace
has always
been at hand.**

Most of us come in contact with spiritual practices and teachings as a result of being dissatisfied with ourselves, or with our circumstances in life.

We want to be less miserable, confused, or stressed, and so we seek a release through spirituality. Maybe we used to seek release from our misery through substances, work, thinking, or any other external condition. In this case, our new seeking may be an improvement compared to our previous way. Our search for peace has now become more refined.

However, at some point we may come to the realization that we are still looking for peace. As if something must happen before we can have peace.

If we examine closely what is happening, we will see that our impulse to find peace, is the exact impulse that keeps us from being peaceful. As long as we follow that impulse, we strengthen it.

When this is seen, we can observe the impulse itself and just allow it to come and go. Peace is not an achievement of, but a returning to. By realizing we were out for a walk, we can return home to awareness. Until we reach a point through practice where we are able to remain home, no matter where we are in the world.

Peace is simply the absence of the urge that seeks it.

**To believe that peace
must be achieved
is to deny peace.**

Perhaps the biggest obstacle for realizing inner peace is the belief that it lies in the future. This belief implies that peace is not yet present, that it must be achieved. As if inner peace is to be found in the horizontal realm.

Think of the horizontal realm as the realm of time, space, and matter; it is where evolution, growth, and cause and effect take place. It is the domain of the phenomenal world of arising and passing, birth and death. It is what in India is called Maya.

The vertical realm is the transcendent realm of pure consciousness, or being. It is unchanging, permanent, uncaused. It is the eternal realm. Eternal, not in the sense that it is ever lasting in time, but meaning timeless, ever present, immediate, right now.

As long as we search for peace in the horizontal realm, we will never find it, and if we do find it, it is short lived, because everything in the horizontal realm is impermanent.

To realize inner peace, all we have to do is realize the eternal in the present moment. Be aware. That which is aware of the time passing is itself timeless. That which is aware of the aging of your body is itself ageless. That which is aware of motion is itself motionless. That which is aware of your distress is itself already peaceful.

Peace never abandons us, it is we who abandon it.

It's not what you do that matters most, It's from what place you do it that matters most.

Someone once asked me, "This inner peace seems great and all, but once I have found it, will I just sit blissfully in a chair for the rest of my time and do nothing?"

The assumption here is that inner peace is some kind of beautiful finish line. But in fact, it is the starting point from which everything that is beautiful originates. When we're at peace, our actions reflect that peace. We bring into being what we radiate, not just what we advocate.

In moments of decision, it is essential to return to the place in our hearts that is ever peaceful; our being.
When we are deeply rooted in being, we become lovers.
If not, we become seekers.

Seeking is propelled by the longing to return home to our being. Compassion is the natural result of being rooted in being. As we are rooted in being, our sense of separateness dissolves. We recognize ourselves and others as unique expressions of one underlying whole. This realization naturally compels us to act in the world from a place of love and compassion.

So if we ever wonder what to do, perhaps the timeless words of Saint Augustine are worth reflecting on,
"Love, and do what you will. If you hold your peace, hold your peace out of love. If you cry out, cry out in love. If you correct someone, correct them out of love. If you spare them, spare them out of love. Let the root of love be in you: nothing can spring from it but good."[50]

**The question is not,
"How do you want
to be remembered?"**

**The question is,
"Why do you want
to be remembered?"**

In the summer of 2020, during a dinner at my mentor's home, I realized he would soon pass away as his physical health was quickly declining due to his cancer. I asked him, 'How do you want to be remembered?' He burst out laughing with a cosmic laugh and replied, "Why should I want to be remembered?"

His answer made me laugh as well. And as I'm writing down these memories, it's not the messenger but the message that I remember most.

In my own spiritual pursuits, he always encouraged me not to look for what is missing, but to look for what is ever present. That which is so near that it cannot be seen. He invited me to find what was never lost.

My teacher was often in great physical pain, yet I rarely noticed a trace of despair or aversion in him. In his eyes I could only see peace and surrender.

Sometimes, during our talks, I suddenly felt Home. Not the house I was born in, but the eternal Home with a capital H. A place we arrive when our longing to be elsewhere is gone. In fact, it's not even a place you arrive. It's an ever present reality where "you" dissolve into. It is experienced as the "peace that surpasses understanding." I call it Home.

Perhaps the point is not to live so that people remember us. Perhaps the point is to live so that through our presence, people remember Home.

"We are all just walking each other home." – Ram Dass[51]

Notes

1. T. S. Eliot, 'Little Gidding', *Four Quartets* (Faber and Faber 1944)
2. Psalm 46:10. The word God used to trigger all sorts of negative associations in me, but these days it awakens inspiration in me; a sense of ultimacy. If the word triggers negative associations in you, feel free to replace it with Being or Ultimate Reality.
3. Rumi, *Selected Poems*, translated by Coleman Barks, (Castle Books 1997), p. 109
4. Steven Taylor, *Extraordinary Awakenings* (New world Library 2021)
5. "A man with outward courage dares to die, a man with inward courage dares to live." Witter Bynner, *The way of life*, according to Lao Tzu, an American version (Penguin 1986), p. 101
6. Widely used paraphrase of the quote "The opposite of addiction isn't sobriety. It's connection." Johann Hari, *Chasing the Scream: The First and Last Days of the War on Drugs* (Bloomsbury USA 2016), p. 293
7. G. K. Chesterton, *Orthodoxy* (John Lane 1909), p. 32
8. This case is beautifully made in the following book:. Iain McGilchrist, *The master and his emissary* (Yale University Press 2012)
9. Slavoj Žižek, *The sublime object of ideology* (Verso 2008), p. 23
10. M. K. Ghandi, *The story of my experiments with truth*, translated by Mahadev Desai, edited by Tripid Suhrud (Yale University Press 2018), p. 436
11. Lao Tzu, *Tao te Ching*, translated by Wing-Tsit Chan (Pearson 1963), chapter 67.
12. Widely attributed to Jung. Sometimes translated as 'Neurosis is always a substitute for legitimate suffering.' From *Psychology and Religion*, Yale University press 1938), p. 92
13. Mooji, *Before I am*, (Mooji Media 2012), pp. 31-38
14. G.I. Gurdjieff, *Views from the real world* (1973), p. 240
15. John Welwood, Toward a psychology of awakening (Shambhala 2002)
16. C. G. Jung, *Modern Man in Search of a Soul* (Kegan Paul Trench Trubner and Co 1933), p. 285
17. Jesus. *The Gospel of Thomas*, Saying 70. The Gospel of Thomas is not part of the Bible. It was discovered near Nag Hammadi in 1945 among a group of books known as the Nag Hammadi library.
18. H.W.L. Poonja, *This: prose and poetry on dancing emptiness* (Weiser Books 2000), p. 51
19. See for example Pierre Hadot, *Philosophy as a way of life* (Wiley Blackwell 1995)
20. André Chastel, The Renaissance: *Essays in Interpretation* (Methuen 1982), p. 107
21. Gunilla Norris, *Inviting silence: Universal principles of Meditation* (BlueBridge 2004), p. 7
22. Gary Snyder, *The Practice of the Wild; Essays by Gary Snyder* (North Point Press 1990), p. 7
23. Lin Yutang, *The importance of living* (Reynal & Hitchcock 1937), p. 150
24. Richard Rohr, *Falling Upward: A Spirituality for the Two Halves of Life* (Jossey-Bass 2011). Introduction, p. 17
25. Meister Eckhart, *The complete mystical works of Meister Eckhart*, translated by Maurice O'C Walshe (The Crossroad Publishing Company 2009), p. 492

26. Widely attributed to Albert Einstein
27. Popular translation of "I have discovered that all the unhappiness of men arises from one single fact, that they cannot stay quietly in their own chamber." Blaise Pascal, *Pensées* (Random House 1941), p. 48
28. Hubert van Zeller, *Leave your life alone* (Templegate Publishers 1972)
29. I e-mailed Professor Kreeft for the proper reference, but he could not remember it (he wrote more than 80 books). However, he gave me permission to use his quote.
30. See for example D. C. Schindler, *Freedom from Reality: the diabolical character of modern liberty* (University of Notre Dame Press 2017)
31. Lao Tzu, *Tao te Ching*, translated by Stephen Mitchell (Harper Collins 2006), chapter 71
32. William Blake, *The marriage of heaven and hell* (Dover Publications 1994), p. 36
33. Lao Tzu, *Tao te Ching*, translated by Stephen Mitchell (Harper Collins 2006), chapter 1
34. Retrieved from World of Proverbs. [www.worldofproverbs.com]
35. Eckhart Tolle, *Stillness speaks* (New World library 2003), ch 1, p. 3
36. See for example Marie-Louise von Franz, *The problem of the Puer Aeternus* (Inner City Books 2000)
37. Dōgen Zenji as quoted in Jakusho Kwong, *No Beginning, No End: The Intimate Heart of Zen* (Harmony Books 2003), p. 175
38. Although this teaching is present in many traditions, this realization became most clear to me by studying the works of Rupert Spira. Rupert's teachings have influenced me deeply. See for example Rupert Spira, *The heart of prayer* (Sahaya Publications 2023)
39. Rumi, *The Rumi Collection; an anthology of translations of Mevlâna Jalâluddin Rimu*, edited by Kabir Helminski (Shambhala 2005), p. 112
40. Lin Yutang, *The importance of living* (Reynal & Hitchcock 1937), p. 10
41. See 'hexagram 60', *I ching, the book of change*.
42. Nisargadatta Maharaj, *I am That* (The Acorn Press 1973), p. 204
43. Erich Fromm, *To have or to be* (Continuum 2008)
44. Erich Fromm, *To have or to be* (Continuum 2008), p. 89
45. Sigmund Freud, 'Letter to Marie Bonaparte, August 1937', *The letters of Sigmund Freud* (Basic Books 1975), p. 436
46. See: https://www.youtube.com/watch?v=UoQdp2prfmM&t=0s timestamp: 37:58. Dr. Peterson attributes the quote to Carl Jung, but I could not find the quote in Jung's collected works.
47. Jean Klein, *I am* (Non-duality press 2006), back cover.
48. Ludwig Wittgenstein, *Tractatus Logico-Philosophicus*, Translated by D. F. Pears and B. F. McGuinness (Routledge 2002), p. 87
49. Bodhidharma, *The Zen Teaching of Bodhidharma* (North Point Press 2009,) p. 5
50. Saint Augustine, *Homilies on the First Epistle of John*, Sermon 8 (407 AD)
51. Widely attributed to Ram Dass.

About the author

From a young age, Alexander den Heijer has been fascinated by existential questions such as 'What am I?" and, "How to live well?" These questions have sent him on an endless spiritual quest to understand himself and the world he lives in. He has been exploring the philosophies and teachings of many spiritual traditions. He loves sharing his findings along the way through writing and public speaking. He is also frequently hired by organizations to explore how these teachings can be applied to enhance organizational cultures. Alexander lives in Amsterdam.

Printed in Great Britain
by Amazon